Printed and bound by
FOOTE & DAVIES, INC.
Atlanta, Georgia

UNITED STATES
NAVAL TRAINING CENTER

GREAT LAKES, ILL.

HISTORY OF THE UNITED STATES NAVAL TRAINING CENTER

GREAT LAKES, ILL.

Great Lakes is your Navy's largest Training Center.

The Center was first a Naval Training Station, provided for in the Naval Appropriation Act of April 27, 1904, which authorized the President to appoint a board to select a site on the Great Lakes, to purchase and to establish a Naval Training Station.

The board investigated 37 possible locations, among them the 172-acre Lake Bluff, Illinois site which consisted of 120 acres known as the Joseph Downey farm and 52 acres owned by William H. Murphy. Asking price for these two tracts was $1,000 per acre.

The Merchants' Club of Chicago conducted a successful fund-raising campaign to provide money for purchasing the property, and offered the property as a gift to the Government from the people of Chicago. The offer was accepted.

On November 24, 1904, the President authorized establishment of the Naval Training Station at the Great Lakes location. Captain, later Rear Admiral, Albert A. Ross, first Commandant, was appointed to supervise construction.

On July 1, 1911—six years to the day after construction began—the station was commissioned, almost four months before it was dedicated.

The completed Station consisted of 39 buildings with a capacity of 1,500 men.

On the bleak and windy afternoon of October 28, 1911, President William Howard Taft stood on an open platform in front of the Administration Building and formally dedicated the Center.

In April 1917, when the United States entered World War I, the Station covered 167 acres and included 33 buildings, exclusive of residences. An expansion program was begun to meet war demands and was continuous throughout the war. On Armistice Day, 1918, the Station covered 1,200 acres, with 775 buildings, and had 45,000 men undergoing training. Over 125,000 men received their first Navy training here in World War I.

From the close of World War I until September 9, 1939, when President Roosevelt proclaimed a national emergency, the Station underwent a period of restricted activity, being completely closed as a training activity from June 30, 1933, to July 29, 1935. On the day the emergency was proclaimed, the total population of the Station was less than 1,000.

July 26, 1940, marked the beginning of a construction program which became the most extensive in Station history.

By Pearl Harbor Day, capacity had been increased to approximately 14,000 billets. The day Japan struck at Pearl Harbor, construction of 32 more barracks, two mess halls and other miscellaneous buildings was authorized. By the following Monday morning, the first group of carpenters and laborers were at work. More than 10,000 civilians worked 24 hours a day, seven days a week. Early in 1942, the Veterans' Administration transferred some 325 acres of land from the Veterans' Hospital for the construction of more training facilities. This addition expanded the Station's capacity 44,000 billets.

On June 16, 1942, the Bureau of Yards and Docks authorized further expansion of training facilities for another 24,000 recruits. On July 7, 1942, a considerable number of parcels of property comprising 685 acres was acquired for the new construction program. On September 21, 1942, all barracks and mess halls in the new area were in commission and occupied.

The U. S. Naval Training Center at Great Lakes trained over 1,000,000 Bluejackets during World War II.

At the present time Great Lakes includes approximately 800 buildings. During the war-time peak some 1,000 buildings were in use, with a crowded capacity of 100,000 and an area of 1,500 acres.

On March 28, 1944, the Training Station was established by Secretary Forrestal as a group command and redesignated as the U. S. Naval Training Center, Great Lakes, Illinois.

A veteran of two World Wars, Great Lakes has served with distinction in its role as a recruit training installation as well as the home of several of the Navy's Service Schools. A major Naval hospital occupies a large portion of the area and boasts complete facilities for maintaining the Navy's high standards of physical efficiency. Also located at Great Lakes is the headquarters of the Commandant, Ninth Naval District.

The Service Schools Command assumes a great importance today as the Navy's knowledge is expanding and the need for more specialists arises. Seven schools are located at Great Lakes in which 2,500 men are constantly enrolled, each learning a trade or perfecting some technical skill. The largest school concerns itself with electronics— including radar. The other schools cover such fields as fire control, machinery, electricity, motor mechanics, etc. Complete laboratories and workshops have been built to assist in making the Service School students well-trained and efficient in their chosen trades.

With the coming of world peace, Great Lakes is assuming a new role as a guardian of that peace. The New Civilian Naval Reserve has been organized to retain the "know-how" and Navy spirit acquired by millions during the recent war. Men now out of uniform who are interested in "keeping their hand in" are volunteering for a short period of active duty at the Naval Training Center during which time they are given the opportunity to brush up on their Navy-learned skills and keep abreast of new developments. Great Lakes is now playing host to many "civilian bluejackets" in an effort to keep a strong and peaceful America.

With the closing of several Naval installations and the consolidation of others, Great Lakes is destined to continue as one of our most vital training installations.

CAPTAIN H. J. GRASSIE, U. S. Navy
Commander, Naval Training Center

CAPTAIN F. J. GRANDFIELD, USN
Commanding Officer
Recruit Training Command

COMMANDER J. D. CROWLEY, USN
Executive Officer
Recruit Training Command

Main entrance to the U. S. Naval Training Center, Great Lakes, Illinois.

VIEWS

A Recruit barracks.

Ship's Service is the Navy's
department store.

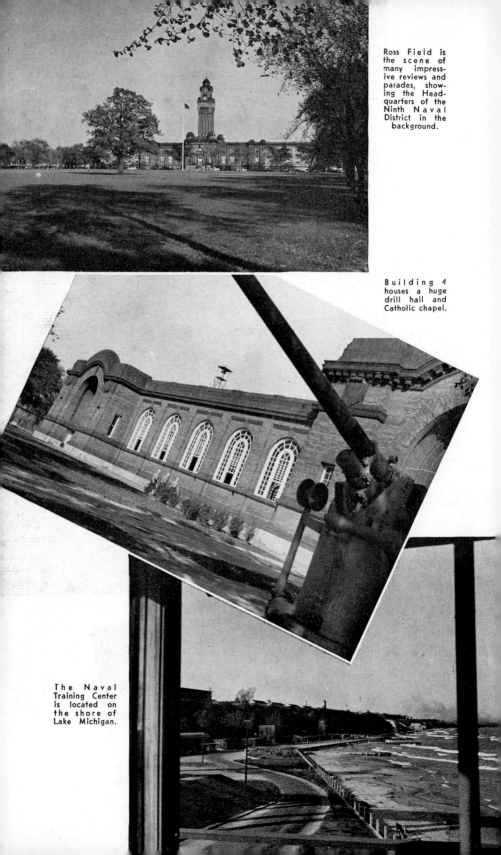

Ross Field is the scene of many impressive reviews and parades, showing the Headquarters of the Ninth Naval District in the background.

Building 4 houses a huge drill hall and Catholic chapel.

The Naval Training Center is located on the shore of Lake Michigan.

A drill hall and gymnasium in Camp Barry.

Recreation Buildings provide off-duty relaxation and entertainment. Complete with gymnasiums, swimming pools, Ship's Service, soda fountains and reading rooms, these buildings are popular during the Recruit's spare time.

Meals are served in modern dining halls.

TRAINING

Top: New Recruits enter Camp Barry at the Naval Training Center
and begin processing.
Bottom: A general view of Camp Barry.

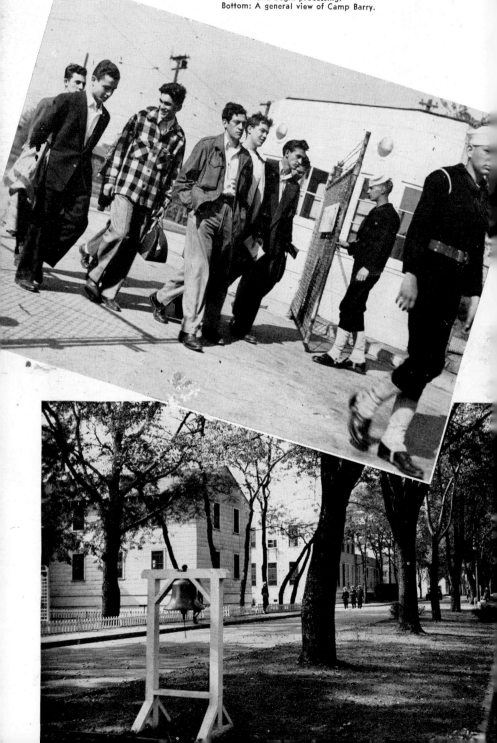

Receiving Unit personnel who process all new Recruits.

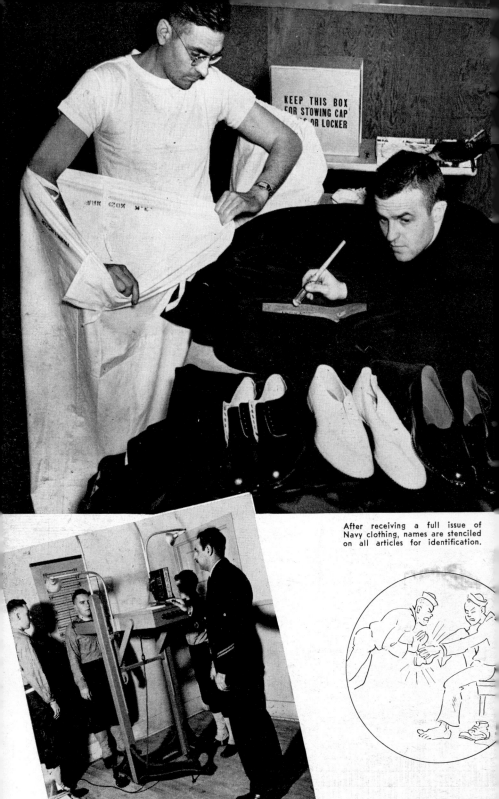

After receiving a full issue of Navy clothing, names are stenciled on all articles for identification.

A photograph is taken of the new Recruit for his identification card.

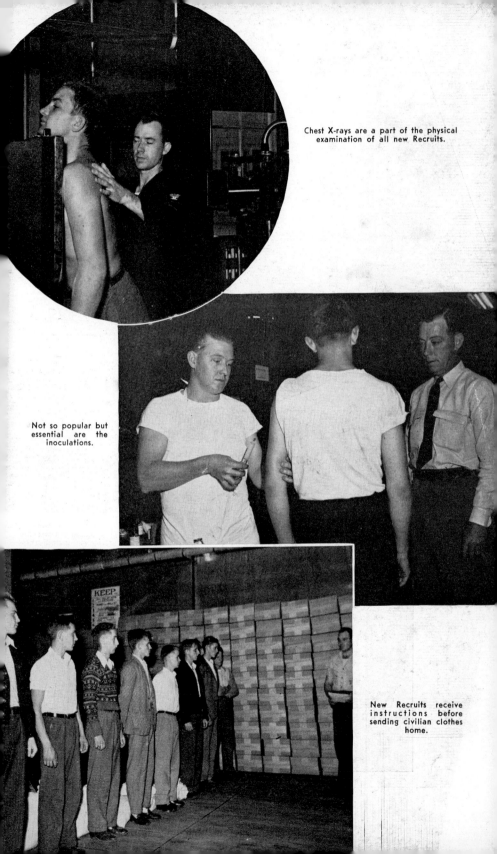

Chest X-rays are a part of the physical examination of all new Recruits.

Not so popular but essential are the inoculations.

New Recruits receive instructions before sending civilian clothes home.

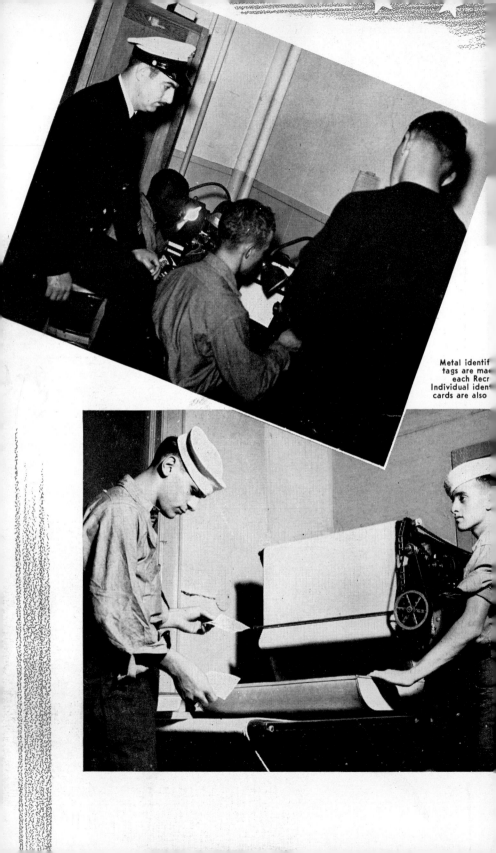

Metal identif
tags are ma
each Recr
Individual iden
cards are also

The Company Commander helps his men to attain the Navy's traditional high standards of appearance.

Recruits are given instruction in the proper way of wearing the Navy uniform. Here a new Recruit is shown how to wear his cap.

A Bluejacket's bedding is aired frequently.

A Company is instructed in the fundamentals of marching. They try it for the first They try it again again and improve with time.

The day's program is outlined
by the Company Commander.

Containing a multitude of information about their new life, the "Bluejackets' Manual" and "Your Navy"
are thoroughly studied by all Recruits.

With space a premium aboard ship, early Navy training teaches the recruit how to roll his clothing in order to conserve the limited space in his seabag.

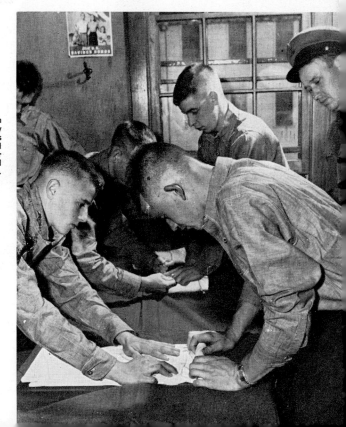

Top: Cleanliness is taught from the beginning. Here Recruits are shown the proper methods of washing their clothing. Bottom: Recruits take pride in cleanliness and neatness . . . even in the appearance of the clothes lines.

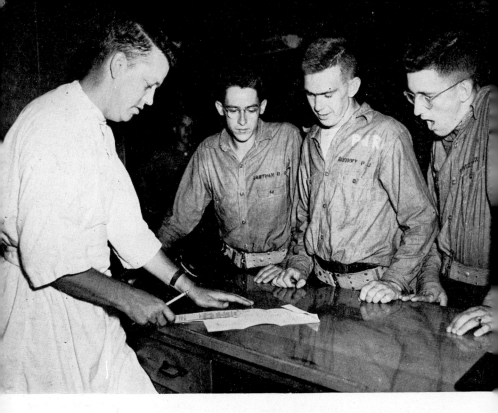

Dental care is available to all Navy men. Navy dental officers offer a complete service for proper treatment and correction.

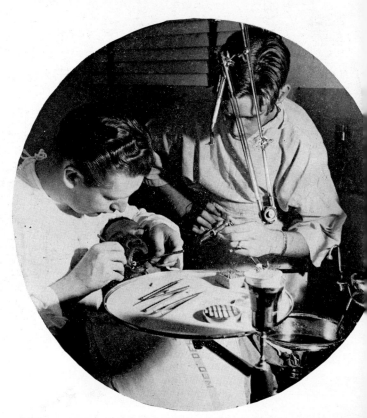

A bulletin board announces the uniform of the day for all Recruits.

Headquarters for the Recruit Training Command, Building E, Camp Barry.

All Recruits are encouraged to pursue the religious faith of their choice. Several are shown here conferring with a Protestant Chaplain.

A Catholic Chaplain also assists Recruits with their problems.

And practice toward perfection continues
on the "grinder."

Recruits move on to advanced
stages of training as they leave
Camp Barry for other sections of
the Naval Training Center.

Entrance to Camps Dewey, Downes, and Porter. Home of the 8th, 10th, and 12th Regiments.

Administration building for 14th Regiment in Camp Moffett.

Recruits entering the barracks which will be their home for the remainder of their training period.

Coordination and physical conditioning are important in the training of the Bluejacket. Many hours are spent on Constitutional Field in order to reach perfection in both.

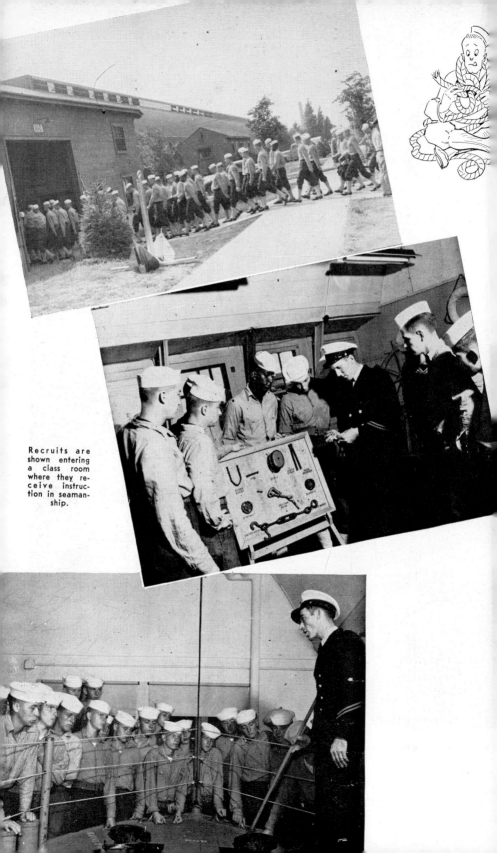

Recruits are shown entering a class room where they receive instruction in seamanship.

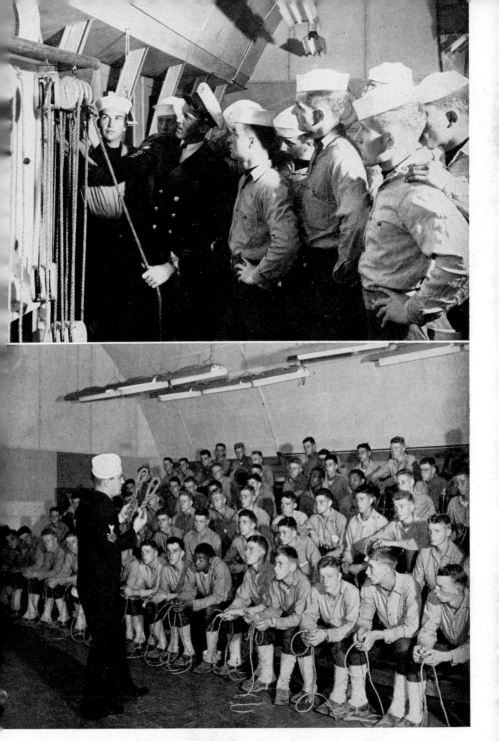

Seamanship training includes instruction in the use of the block and tackle (top) and the tying of knots (bottom.)

A plastic model of an aircraft carrier is used in the seamanship department. Complete in every detail, the model helps Recruits to become familiar with the parts of a Navy ship.

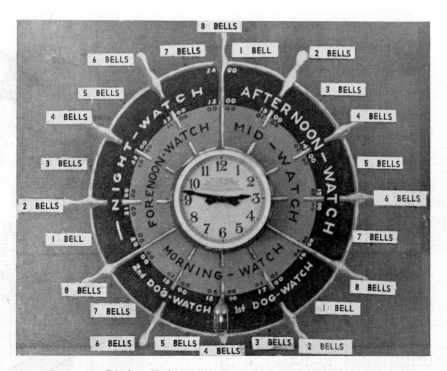

This chart aids the Recruit in learning to tell time Navy style.

Seamanship instruction includes the demonstration of actual equipment on the deck of a mock ship constructed in a classroom.

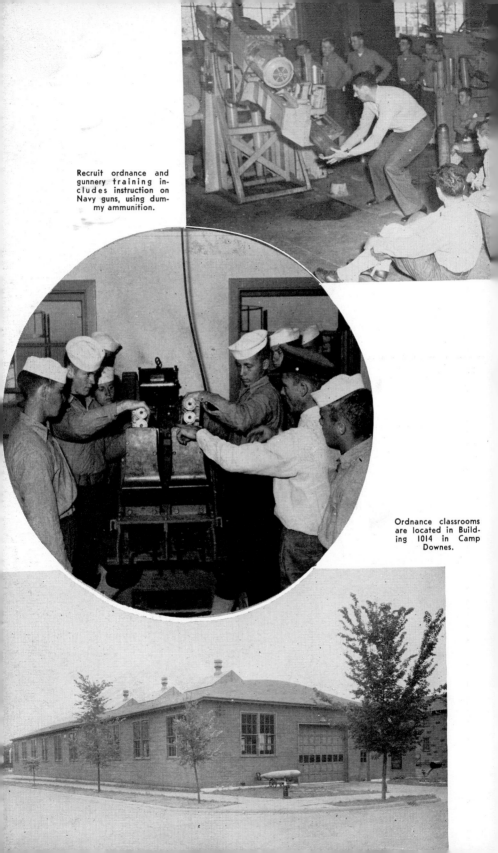

Recruit ordnance and gunnery training includes instruction on Navy guns, using dummy ammunition.

Ordnance classrooms are located in Building 1014 in Camp Downes.

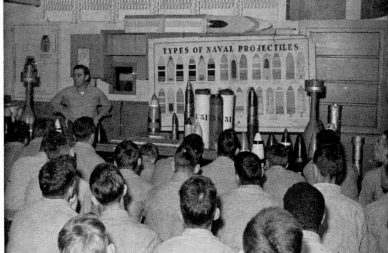

Instructors, in demonstrating the various Naval guns and their projectiles, emphasize safety precautions.

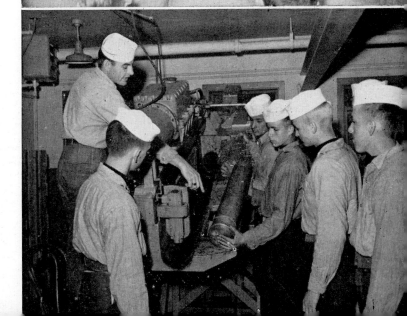

The proper wearing of the gas mask is another subject covered by the Ordnance and Gunnery Department.

During the winter months Recruits fire .22 caliber rifles in the indoor rifle range.

Rifle instruction on the outdoor rifle range.

Firing from various positions is required as Recruits qualify for "Marksman," "Sharpshooter" or "Expert."

While on the range, Recruits alternate between firing and working at the targets. Here they are shown patching and marking the targets.

All activities on the range are supervised by Marine Corps personnel.

All Navy men must be able to swim. Each Recruit must demonstrate his proficiency in the water.

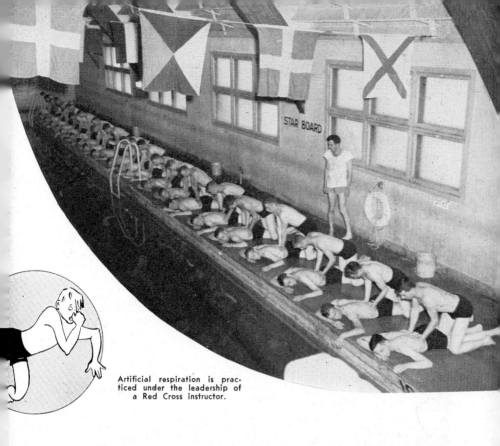

Artificial respiration is prac-
ticed under the leadership of
a Red Cross instructor.

All non-qualified swimmers are given instruction to improve their swimming ability.

An instru... teaches pr... swimming t... niques t... class of ... cruits.

Beginners practice for final test.

A Recruit class ready for instruction.

The start of a race.

Under competent instructors, Recruits are also taught to swim through burning oil in water.

Practicing the "flutter kick."

Healthful exercises
build strong
bodies.

Frequent clothing inspections are held to insure that each Recruit has sufficient equipment and in good condition.

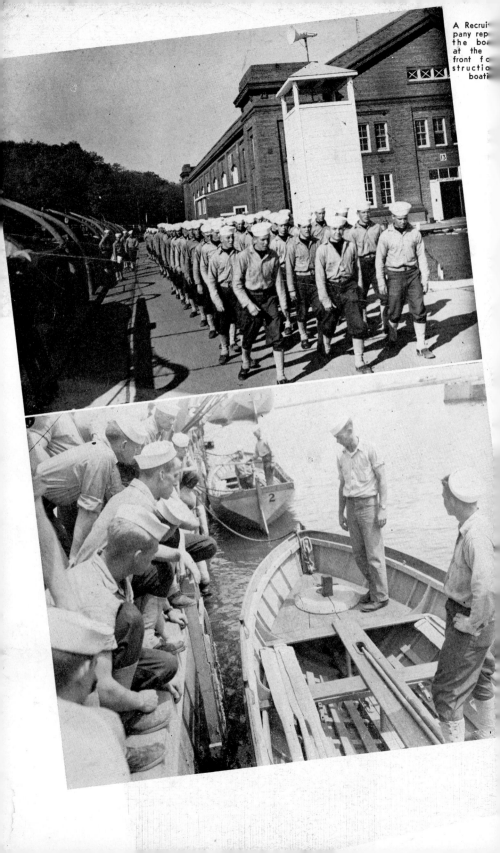

e "taking to
vater," Re-
are taught
to raise and
boats on
davits.

Although no excursion trips, these boating sessions are among the most popular phases of training to the Recruits.

Teamwork and coordination are acquired through boat races and drills.

A day at the Fire Fighters Training Unit teaches Recruits the method of extinguishing all types of fires at sea in a scientific manner.

At the call of "Fire," Recruit fire fighting crews rush into action.

A simulated hangar deck of an aircraft carrier filled with burning oil becomes a classroom for the fire fighters.

Clad in foul weather gear, a Recruit leaves the hangar deck after a blaze is extinguished.

Different types of equipmer are used in combatting var ous kinds of fires. Recruits ar shown here fighting an o blaze.

With actual experience in battling these blazes, the Recruit learns that fire at sea, although danger- ous, can normally be brought under control by employing the proper fire fighting techniques.

Top: To prevent Navy fire fighters from becoming "smoke-eaters," the rescue breathing apparatus was devised to enable them to enter smoke filled compartments safely.

Top: Care and treatment of hose, nozzles and other fire fighting equipment is carefully explained to the Recruit classes.

Bottom: The approved method for extinguishing a particular fire is described to the fire fighting team.

Recruits pass in review during graduation parade on Ross Field.

Top: The Crack Drill Team performs on special occasions. Members practice on their own time after work hours.

Bottom: Recruit Honormen, selected from each graduating Company, are recognized at the graduation reviews and are presented appropriate certificates by Capt. Grandfield and distinguished visitor.

Culminating the intensive training program, these Recruit reviews are colorful ceremonies and are popular with visitors throughout the middle west.

Recruit companies pass in review before the Commandant, Ninth Naval District, and his staff.

Recruit training is over!
Heading for home on
leave!

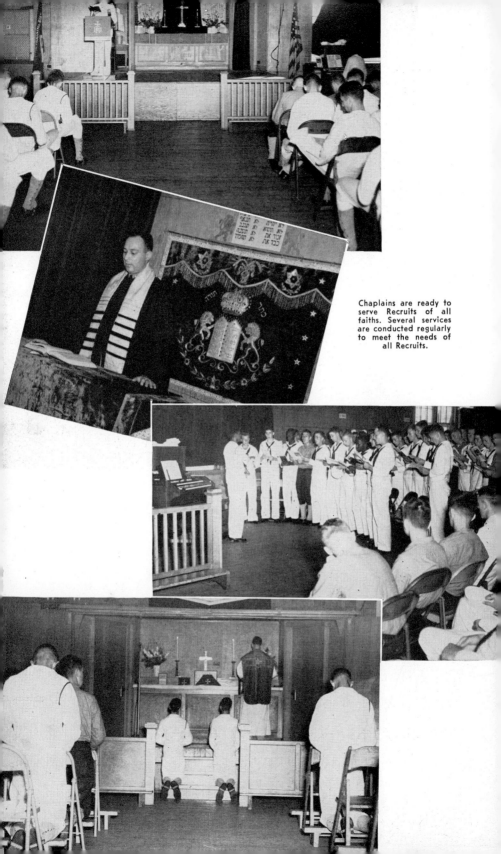

Chaplains are ready to serve Recruits of all faiths. Several services are conducted regularly to meet the needs of all Recruits.

The highlight of the Recruit's stay at Great Lakes is the week-end visitors from home.

Football is part of the entertainment program.

Off station parade.

Already a "salt," the graduating Recruit spins a yarn for the benefit of his feminine admirers.

The staff of the "Great Lakes Bulletin," the Naval Training Center newspaper, selects photographs for next week's issue.

The Recruit Dance Band practices after working hours and always draws a crowd of listeners.

Mail from home!

Fun

and

Recreation

Wholesome meals are served cafeteria style in large mess halls. The Navy's slogan applies "Take all you want—but eat all you take."

A fully equip-
ped hobby shop
affords the Re-
c r u i t m a n y
profitable leis-
ure hours.

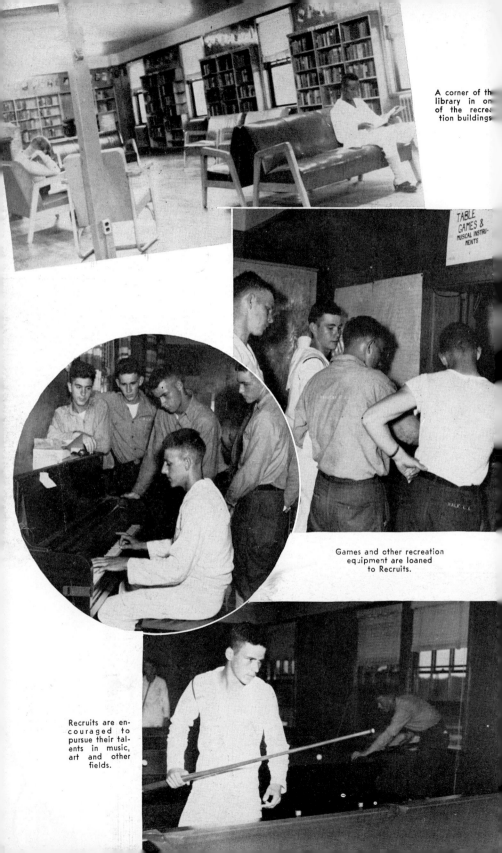

A corner of the library in one of the recreation buildings

TABLE GAMES & MUSICAL INSTRUMENTS

Games and other recreation equipment are loaned to Recruits.

Recruits are encouraged to pursue their talents in music, art and other fields.

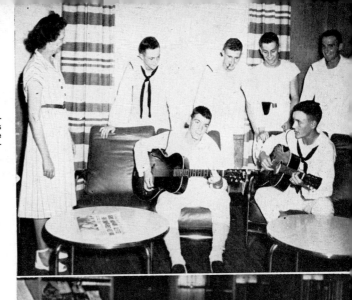

Women leaders organize games and contests and supervise the use of a variety of equipment.

Current magazines and newspapers as well as a large collection of books are to be found in the libraries.

At graduation each company holds a farewell party in one of the recreation centers.

Anchors Aweigh, my boys,

Anchors Aweigh.

Farewell to all these joys,

We sail at break of day.

To our last night on shore,

Drink to the foam.

Until we meet once more,

Here's wishing you a happy voyage home.

COMPANY 398

Company Commander
F. J. WROBEL, B.M.C.

Asst. Company Commander
O. L. DEIBERT, Q.M.C.

eading from left to right: Top Row: John J. Ahern, Jr., Kenneth A. Anderson, William J. Antonicci; Second Row: chard V. Arunski, William D. Bacon, Thomas H. Barstow, James D. Bass, Jack L. Beck, Gerald Bellart, Leo erning, Jr., John W. Biehn; Third Row: Richard E. Billish, Robert W. Birdsong, Harold D. Bishop, James O. Bock, rold W. Boss, Emory L. Bothast, Arnold L. Boyd, Earl L. Boyer; Fourth Row: Joseph K. Bradford, Vernon P. isson, Donald M. Brown, Ray D. Burgess, Theodore G. Cherveny, James M. Clark, Robert L. Conflitti, Glenn E. y; Bottom Row: Bailey M. Crawford, George C. Cutler, George H. Damminga, William F. Daniels, Jack S. Daniel, Nolan P. Delapp, Leonard J. Dicks, Robert K. Dickson.

Reading from left to right: Top Row: Edward A. Doran, Harry J. Druzbik, Lloyd R. Dyer, Samuel E. Dyer, Om
L. Dyer, Warren F. Dyer, Clement C. Felton, Richard W. Fennesy; Second Row: Harold J. Flaugher, Ronald
Flavin, Richard H. Flinn, B. C. Frothingham, Jr., Leslie S. Gagnon, James J. Garland, Jr., Richard E. Gaul
Stanley P. Goff; Third Row: Daniel L. Gordon, Norman G. Grubb, Donald F. Gutschmidt, Eli E. Hager, Alan V
Hamilton, Richard E. Hammond, Leland G. Hartman, Billy R. Hensley; Fourth Row: Richard J. Hildreth, Willia
E. Hooe, William C. Huber, Eugene B. Hughes, Donald J. Hurda, Arthur A. Johannes, Harold H. Johnson, Har
Kolar; Fifth Row: Alvin J. Kucharzyk, Martin W. Lange, Charles A. Lauinger, Laurie L. Leblanc, A. W. Letournea
Jr., James K. Luger, John H. Lynch, Melvin M. Madsen; Sixth Row: Thomas E. Mahaffey, Robert L. Mans, Dan
Maguire, Donald M. Marek, Andrew R. McMaster, A. F. Melenbrink, Burton S. Meyers, Eugene A. Mills; Botto
Row: Raymond E. Moomey, Harold F. Mosier, Jr., Philip D. Neuhauser, Raymond J. Nolte, Jr., William L. Nugen
F. C. Okraszwski, Chester R. Oleske, John P. Pionke.

ading from left to right: Top Row: Richard E. Poulson, William E. Pumphrey, Neil D. Rasmussen, Robert E.
id, Henery P. Riley, Jr., William W. Robinson, William E. Rostagno, Richard C. Rotz; Second Row: John
rdinha, Earl L. Schlafge, Paul M. Scott, James C. Seelen, Edward J. Semla, Lavon H. Severence, Glenn A.
monson, Myron A. Smith; Third Row: Fred L. Smith, Jr., Gerald A. Sorge, Ernest J. Stawarski, Chester F. Stacy,
bert A. Steinmetz, James B. Strom, Ronald V. Sutherland, Louis J. Terborg; Fourth Row: Donald J. Thompson,
cco M. Tommasini, Robert E. Ware, Harry E. Weil, Richard L. Whiting, John F. Woodruff, Edward B. Young,
Howard E. Hoffman; Bottom Row: Courtenay S. Whitman, Bernard H. Denekamp, Derwyn K. Hillier.

Our physical
training pro-
gram keeps us
in top shape.

Our training in
fire fighting
m a y someday
save our lives.

ACTUALLY FIRING

We fire .22 caliber rifles and .45 caliber pistols on the indoor range.

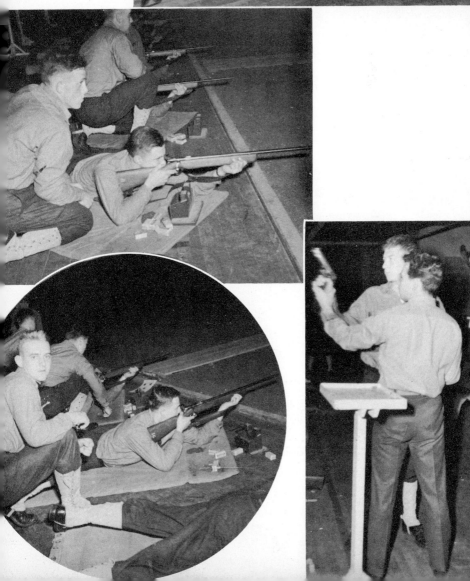

Service week in
the galley.

We drill on the
regimental
"grinder."

A good part of
our time is
spent in the
classroom where
we study many
subjects.